'An instruction manual in intellectual duplicity
that no aspiring parliamentarian, trainee lawyer,
wannabe TV interviewer or newspaper columnist
can afford to be without.'

New Statesman

'Purchasers should be careful to whom they give
this book.'

Financial Times

'Obviously engaging... I wish I had read it
earlier... [a] perfectly formed volume, warmly
recommended.'

Isabelle Hilton presenting *Nightwaves BBC Radio 3*

The Art of
Always Being Right

By

Arthur Schopenhauer

GIBSON SQUARE

Introduced by
A.C. Grayling

Published by
Gibson Square Books Ltd
15 Gibson Square, London N1 0RD
Tel: +44 (0)20 7689 4790; Fax: +44 (0)20 7689 7395
info@gibsonsquare.com
www.gibsonsquare.com

ISBN 1-903933-61-7

2005, 2nd printing

Sales by Signature
Castlegate 20, York YO1 9RP
Tel 01904 633 633; Fax 01904 675 445
sales@signaturebooks.co.uk
www.signaturebooks.co.uk

UK, Ireland & Europe distribution by Central Books Ltd
99 Wallis Road, UK London E9 5LN
Tel +44 (0)845 458 9911; Fax +44 (0)845 458 9912
info@centralbooks.com
www.centralbooks.com

Australian, New Zealand, Canada, South Africa, US sales,
please contact Gibson Square Books Ltd.

Index

Contents

Contents

Introduction

Introduction

A.C. Grayling

When Schopenhauer wrote his essay 'The Art of Always Being Right', did he intend it to be an exercise in irony? It offers pungent practical advice on how to beat an adversary in debate, and the advice it gives is unapologetically Machiavellian. 'Controversial dialectic', he writes, 'is the art of disputing, and of disputing in such a way as to hold one's own, whether one is right or wrong.' He here deliberately—and if non-ironically, then provocatively—echoes those sophists of classical antiquity who, on the negative view of them encouraged by Socrates and Plato, offered to teach anyone the art of making the worst case seem the better and the better case seem the worst, independently of truth and justice—and for a fee.

Socrates and Plato accordingly had nothing but contempt for sophistry thus understood. The targets of their endeavours were truth and the good, and they distinguished between what they called 'dialectic', which for them consisted in sincere inquiry effected by means of question, answer and discussion, and the sophists' use of rhetorical devices and emotional appeals for purposes merely of persuasion. Since rhetoric had only persuasion as its end, it had no place for analysis and critical examination of ideas. Sophists were able to teach their skills for money because these skills were much in demand in classical antiquity, where eloquence and success in debate were the cruces on which individual fortunes turned. It was the profoundly unethical nature of the enterprise and its motivations, as they saw it, that invited the scorn of Plato and his teacher; and the taint they imputed to it has coloured all subsequent history's view of the sophists, whose rhetorical and suasive arts to this day have a bad name—the name, already pejoratively used, of 'sophistry'.

And yet this is exactly what Schopenhauer offers to teach in 'The Art of Always Being Right'. As a philosopher, a responsible intellect, a man for whom sympathy and compassion are the fundamentals of morality, can he be serious when he says, 'in debating we must put objective truth aside, or rather, we must regard it as an accidental circumstance, and look only to the defence of our own position and the refutation of our opponent's'? When he talks of 'tricks' by which to defeat an opponent's view whether or not it is true, surely he is warning us against the tricks that unscrupulous opponents might use against us?

The answer is not quite as clear cut as one might like, at least as it applies to the time at which Schopenhauer wrote the essay. Its first English translator, Bailey Saunders, simply assumed that at least the 'sophistical' part of 'The Art of Always Being Right' was ironic in intent. But Schopenhauer was a complex man, and the profoundly bleak vein of pessimism that runs through his thought, coupled with the isolation and lack of regard he suffered for most of his life—a resented exclusion from the comforts and honours of a university position, which made him hostile to 'professors' and always ready to attack them for what he saw as their narrowness and smugness-induced lack of intelligence—makes it hard to dismiss the possibility that he was more than half serious, and perhaps entirely serious, in offering a weapon to those who could oppose and defeat them.

Thus Schopenhauer says, 'A man may be objectively in the right, and nevertheless in the eyes of bystanders, and sometimes in his own, he may come off worst.' Therefore it is well to know how to overcome an adversary in cases where one appears to have the worst of the argument, though being in the right. But that will entail also being able to overcome an adversary even when one is not right.

How can it be that people should argue with an eye to victory, irrespective of truth? 'Simple', says Schopenhauer; it is 'the natural baseness of human nature.' This is the result of 'innate vanity' and the fact that people do not think before they speak, but are loquacious and dishonest—they leap to adopt a position, which they thereafter stick to, independently of whether they know it to be right or wrong, from pride and stubbornness. Vanity always outweighs truth.

Yet—so Schopenhauer continues—'this very dishonesty, this persistence in a proposition which seems false even to ourselves, has something to be said for it'—this time for another reason, and one about which Schopenhauer is perfectly serious. It is that it often happens that we begin with a conviction of being right, but are then made insecure in that conviction by the force of the opponent's argument, only to discover in due course that we were right after all. So it is good to stick to one's guns. 'Thus it is', Schopenhauer observes, 'that the weakness of our intellect and the perversity of our will lend each other mutual support.'

Schopenhauer took it that there was nothing, at least in modern times, comparable to his treatise on sophistical means of winning arguments. But he did not publish it. Instead, later in life, he published the introductory portion of it, significantly revised, in the second volume of his *Parerga and Paralipomena*. Here, as befits this work's epigraph from Juvenal—*vitam impendere vero*, 'dedicate life to truth'—he consciously disavows any Machiavellian intent. Speaking of the essay he now says, 'I had, therefore, compiled and worked out some forty of these stratagems [for winning arguments]. But now I dislike throwing light on all these lurking places of narrow-mindedness and incapacity that are so closely allied to obstinacy, vanity and dishonesty.' Rather than giving tips on how to win arguments, he instead enjoined 'avoiding arguments with the common ruck of people.'* Arguing with them only tempts one into unfairness, sophism and chicanery (all three of these words are his own), and the result is 'always detestable'.

This certainly says that when Schopenhauer looked back on 'The Art of Always Being Right' he saw it as an ironical document, a warning by example rather than precept. And at the time he wrote it his tongue must often have been in his cheek too, for the sheer bald-facedness of some of the tricks he describes. But in so far as it is an angry document too, premising the baseness and self-servingness of human nature, and bluntly offering techniques for outwitting it, the writing of the essay cannot have been altogether tongue-in-cheek.

But Schopenhauer did not publish it in its original unqualified, savage version, and when it appeared posthumously in full it had the protection of his remarks in the *Parerga and Paralipomena*. No-one therefore thinks that Schopenhauer was a genuine Machiavel, purveying dark arts of dishonest argumentation. Instead they see this odd, amusing and enticing little essay as one of the wayward expressions of his genius, and oddly conformable—especially as irony—to the rest of his philosophical outlook.

---

* *Parerga and Paralipomena*, vol. II p. 31.

The Art of
Always Being Right

The Art of
Always Being Right

The art of controversy is the art of disputing
in such a way as to hold one's own, whether
one is in the right or the wrong.[1] A man may
be objectively in the right, and nevertheless
in the eyes of bystanders, and sometimes in
his own, he may come off worst.

For example, I may advance a proof of
some assertion, and my adversary may refute
the proof, and thus appear to have refuted the
assertion. There may, nevertheless, be other
proofs. In this case, of course, my adversary
and I change places. He comes off best,
although, as a matter of fact, he is in the
wrong.

If the reader asks how this is, I reply that it is simply the natural baseness of human nature.

If human nature were not base, but thoroughly honourable, we should in every debate have no other aim than the discovery of truth. We should not in the least care whether the truth proves to be in favour of the opinion which we had begun by expressing, or of the opinion of our adversary. That we should regard as a matter of no importance, or, at any rate, of very secondary consequence.

But, as things are, it is the main concern. Our innate vanity, which is particularly sensitive in reference to our intellectual powers, will not allow that our first position was wrong and our adversary's right.

The way out of this difficulty would be simply to take the trouble always to form a correct judgement.

For this a man would have to think before he spoke. But, with most men, innate vanity is accompanied by loquacity and innate dishonesty. They speak before they think; and even though they may afterwards perceive that they are wrong they want it to seem the contrary. The interest in truth, which may be presumed to have been their only motive when they stated the proposition alleged to be true, now gives way to the interests of vanity.

So, for the sake of vanity, what is true must seem false, and what is false must seem true.

✳ ✳ ✳

Nonetheless, this very dishonesty, this persistence in a proposition which seems false even to ourselves, has something to be said for it.

It often happens that we begin with the firm conviction of the truth of our statement. Then our opponent's argument appears to refute it. Should we abandon our position at once, we may discover later on that we were right after all. The proof we offered was false, but nevertheless there was a proof for our statement which was true. The argument which would have been our salvation did not occur to us at the moment.

Hence we make it a rule to attack a counter-argument—even though to all appearances it is true and cogent—in the belief that its truth is only superficial and that, in the course of the debate, another argument will occur to us by which we may upset it, or succeed in confirming the truth of our statement.

In this way we are almost compelled to become dishonest. At any rate, the temptation to do so is very great. The weakness of our intellect and the perversity of our will lend each other mutual support.

Generally, a disputant fights not for truth, but for his proposition, as though it were a battle on life and death. He sets to work *whether right or wrong*.

Actually, as we have seen, he cannot easily do otherwise. As a rule, then, every man will insist on maintaining whatever he has said, even though for the moment he may consider it false or doubtful.[2]

To some extent everyone is armed by his own cunning and villainy—as revealed by daily experience. Everyone has his natural dialectic, just as he has his natural logic. But his dialectic is by no means as safe a guide as his logic.

It is not so easy for anyone to think or draw an inference contrary to the laws of logic. False judgements are frequent—false conclusions very rare.

A man cannot easily be deficient in natural logic, but he may very easily be deficient in natural dialectic, which is a gift apportioned in unequal measure. In so far natural dialectic resembles the faculty of judgement, which differs in degree with every man. Reason, strictly speaking, is the same. It often happens that in a matter in which a man is really in the right, he is confounded or refuted by merely superficial arguments. If he emerges victorious from a contest, he owes it very often not so much to the correctness of his judgement in stating his proposition, as to the cunning and address with which he defended it.

As in all other cases, the best gifts are born with a man. Nevertheless, much may be done to make him a master of this art by practice, and also by a consideration of the tactics which may be used to defeat an opponent, or which he uses for a similar purpose.

Therefore, even though logic may be of no very real, practical use, dialectic may certainly be so

We must always keep the subject of one branch of knowledge quite distinct from that of any other. To form a clear idea of the province of dialectic, we must pay no attention to objective truth, which is an affair of logic. We must regard it simply as *the art of getting the best of it in a dispute* (which is all the easier if we are actually in the right).

In itself the study of dialectic has nothing to do but to show how a man may defend himself against attacks of every kind, and especially against dishonest attacks. In the same fashion, how he may attack another man's statement without contradicting himself, or generally without being defeated. The discovery of objective truth must be separated from the art of winning acceptance for propositions. Objective truth is an entirely different matter. It is the business of sound judgement, reflection and experience, for which there is no special art.

This, then, is the aim of dialectic. It has

been defined as the logic of appearance; but that definition is a wrong one, as in that case it could only be used to repel false propositions.

Even when a man has truth on his side, he needs dialectic in order to defend and maintain it; he must know what the dishonest tricks are, in order to meet them. In fact, he must often make use of them himself, so as to beat the enemy with his own weapons.

Accordingly, in a dialectical contest we must regard objective truth as an accidental circumstance, and look only to the defence of our own position and the refutation of our opponent's. Truth is in the depths. At the beginning of a contest each man believes, as a rule, that right is on his side; in the course of it, both become doubtful, and the truth is not determined or confirmed until the close.

Dialectic, then, has as little to do with truth as the fencing master considers who is in the right when a quarrel leads to a duel. Thrust and parry is the whole business. It is the art of intellectual fencing: and it is only when we so regard it that we can erect it into a branch of knowledge.[3]

Dialectic in this sense of the word has no other aim but to reduce to a regular system and collect and exhibit the arts which most men employ when they observe, in a dispute, that truth is not on their side, and still attempt to gain the day.

The science of dialectic, in one sense of the word, is mainly concerned to tabulate and analyse dishonest stratagems, in order that in a real debate they may be at once recognised and defeated.

I am not aware that anything has been done in this direction, although I have made inquiries far and wide.[4] It is, therefore, an uncultivated soil. To accomplish our purpose, we must draw from our experience: we must observe how in the debates which often arise in our intercourse with our fellow-men this or that stratagem is employed by one side or the other.

By finding out the common elements in tricks repeated in different forms, we shall be enabled to exhibit certain general stratagems which may be advantageous, as well for our own use, as for frustrating others if they use them.

What follows is to be regarded as a first attempt.

[1] Aristotle does, indeed, distinguish between (i) *logic* as the theory or method of arriving at true conclusions; and (ii) *dialectic* as the method of arriving at conclusions that are accepted —conclusions in regard to which it is not taken for granted that they are false and also not taken for granted that they are true in themselves. What is this but the art of being in the right, whether one has any reason for being so or not, in other words, the art of attaining the appearance of truth, regardless of its substance?

Aristotle divides all conclusions into logical and dialectical, in the manner described, and then into eristical. (iii) *eristic* is the method by which the form of the conclusion is correct, but the premises (the materials from which it is drawn) are not true, but only appear to be true. Finally (iv) *sophistic* is the method in which the form of the conclusion is false, although it seems correct.

These three last properly belong to the art of controversial dialectic, as they have no objective truth in view, but only the appearance of it, and pay no regard to truth itself; that is to say, they aim at victory.

[2] Machiavelli advises his Prince to make use of every moment that his neighbour is weak to attack him; otherwise his neighbour may do the same. If honour and fidelity prevailed in the world, it would be a different matter. But as these are qualities not to be expected, a man must not practise them himself, because he will meet with a bad return. It is just the same in a dispute.

If I allow that my opponent is right as soon as he seems to be so, it is scarcely probable that he will do the same when the position is reversed. As he acts wrongly, I am compelled to act wrongly too. It is easy to say that we must yield to truth. But we cannot assume that our opponent will do it, and therefore we cannot do it either. In fact, if I were to abandon the position on which I had previously bestowed much thought, as soon as it appeared that he was right, it might easily happen that I might be misled by a momentary impression, and give up the truth in order to accept an error.

³ If we take purely objective truth as our aim, we are reduced to mere logic; if we take the honing of false propositions, it is mere sophistic: and in either case it would have to be assumed that we were aware of what was true and what was false: and it is seldom that we have any clear idea of the truth beforehand. The true conception of dialectic is that which we have formed: it is the art of intellectual fencing used for the purpose of getting the best of it in a dispute: and, although the name *eristic* would be more suitable, it is more correct to call it controversial dialectic.

⁴ Two men often engage in a lively dispute, and then return to their homes each of the other's opinion, which he has exchanged for his own. It is easy to say that in every dispute we should have no other aim than the advancement of truth; but before dispute no one knows where it is, and through his opponent's arguments and his own a man is misled.

1

❧❦

Extension

This consists in carrying your opponent's proposition beyond its natural limits—in giving it as general a signification and as wide a sense as possible, so as to exaggerate it. And, on the other hand, in giving your own proposition as restricted a sense and as narrow limits as you can, because the more general a statement becomes, the more numerous are the objections to which it is open.

The defence consists in an accurate statement of the point or essential question at issue.

Example 1
I say that the English were supreme in drama.

My opponent attempts to give an instance to the contrary, and replies that it is a well-known fact that in music, and consequently in opera, they could do nothing at all. I repel the attack by reminding him that music is not included in dramatic art, which includes tragedy and comedy alone. This he knew very well. What he did was try to generalise my proposition so that it would apply to all theatrical representations, and, consequently, to opera and then to music, in order to defeat me.

Contrarily, we may save our proposition by reducing it within narrower limits than we had first intended, if our way of expressing it favours this expedient.

Example 2

A declares that the Peace of 1814 gave back their independence to all the German towns of the Hanseatic League. B gives an instance to the contrary by reciting the fact that Dantzig, which received its independence from Buonaparte, lost it by that Peace. A saves himself thus: 'I said "all German towns", and Dantzig was in Poland.'

Extension

Example 3

Lamarck states that the polyp has no feeling, because it has no nerves. It is certain, however, that it has some sort of perception; for it advances towards light by moving in an ingenious fashion from branch to branch, and it seizes its prey. Hence it has been assumed that its nervous system is spread over the whole of its body in equal measure, as though it were blended with it; for it is obvious that the polyp possesses some faculty of perception without having any separate organs of sense. Since this assumption refutes Lamarck's position, he argues:

> *In that case all parts of its body must be capable of every kind of feeling, and also of motion, of will, of thought. The polype would have all the organs of the most perfect animal in every point of its body; every point could see, smell, taste, hear, and so on; in fact, it could think, judge, and draw conclusions; every particle of its body would be a perfect animal, and it would stand higher than man, as every part of it would possess all the faculties*

which man possesses only in the whole of him. Further, there would be no reason for not extending what is true of the polype to all monads, the most imperfect of all creatures, and ultimately to the plants, which are also alive, etc., etc.

By using dialectical tricks of this kind a writer betrays that he is secretly conscious of being in the wrong. Because it was said that the creature's whole body is sensitive to light, and is therefore possessed of nerves, he makes out that its whole body is capable of thought.

2

❧

Homonyms

This trick is to extend a proposition to something which has little or nothing in common with the matter in question but the similarity of the word—then to refute it triumphantly, and so claim credit for having refuted the original statement.

It may be noted here that synonyms are two words for the same conception; homonyms, two conceptions which are covered by the same word. 'Deep', 'cutting', 'high', used at one moment of bodies, at another of tones, are homonyms; 'honourable' and 'honest' are synonyms.

Every light can be extinguished.
The intellect is a light.
Therefore it can be extinguished.

Here it is at once clear that there are four terms in the syllogism, 'light' being used both in a real and in a metaphorical sense. But if the sophism takes a subtle form, it is, of course, apt to mislead, especially where the conceptions which are covered by the same word are related, and inclined to be inter-changeable.

It is never subtle enough to deceive if it is used intentionally; and therefore cases of it must be collected from actual and individual experience. It would be a very good thing if every trick could receive some short and obviously appropriate name, so that when a man used this or that particular trick, he could be at once reproached for it.

I will give two examples of the homonymy.

Example 1

A: 'You are not yet initiated into the mysteries of the Kantian philosophy.'

B: 'Oh, if it's mysteries you're talking of, I'll have nothing to do with them.'

Example 2

I condemn the principle involved in the word *honour* as a foolish one. For, according to it, a man loses his honour by receiving an insult, which he cannot wipe out unless he replies with a still greater insult or by shedding his adversary's blood or his own. I argue that a man's true honour cannot be outraged by what he suffers, but only and alone by what he does—for there is no saying what may befall any one of us.

My opponent immediately attacks the reason I give and triumphantly proves to me that when a tradesman is falsely accused of misrepresentation, dishonesty, or neglect in his business, it is an attack upon his honour. In that case it was outraged solely by what he suffered, and he could only retrieve it by punishing his aggressor and making him retract.

Here, by a homonym, he was foisting *civic honour*, which is otherwise called *good name*, and which may be outraged by libel and slander, on to the conception of *knightly honour*, also called *point d'honneur*, which may be outraged by insult. And since an attack on the former cannot be disregarded, but must be repelled by public disproof, so, with the same justification, an attack on the latter must not be disregarded either, but it must be defeated by still greater insult and a duel. Here we have a confusion of two essentially different things through the homonymy in the word 'honour', and a consequent alteration of the point in dispute

3

❧

Generalise your opponent's specific statements

Another trick is to take a proposition, which is in reference to some particular matter, as though it were uttered with a general or absolute application. Or, at least, to take it in some quite different sense, and then refute it. Aristotle's example is as follows:

> A Moor is black; but in regard to his teeth he is white; therefore, he is black and not black at the same moment.

This is an obvious sophism, which will deceive no one.

Let us contrast it with one drawn from

actual experience.

In talking of philosophy, I admitted that my system upheld the Quietists, and commended them. Shortly afterwards the conversation turned upon Hegel, and I maintain that his writings were mostly nonsense; or, at any rate, that there were many passages in them where the author wrote the words, and it was left to the reader to find a meaning for them. My opponent did not attempt to refute this assertion, but contented himself by telling me that I had just been praising the Quietists, and that they had written a good deal of nonsense too.

This I admitted. But, by way of correcting him, I said that I had praised the Quietists, not as philosophers and writers, that is to say, for their achievements in the sphere of *theory*, but only as men, and for their conduct in mere matters of *practice*; and that in Hegel's case we were talking of theories. In this way I parried the attack.

These first three tricks are of a kindred charac-
ter. They have in common that something dif-
ferent is attacked from that which was asserted.
In all the examples that I have given, what the
opponent says is true, but it stands in apparent
and not in real contradiction with the thesis. All
that the man whom he is attacking has to do is
to deny the validity of the conclusion which he
draws (that because his proposition is true, ours
is false). In this way his refutation is itself direct-
ly refuted by a denial of his conclusion.

❈ ❈ ❈

Another trick is to refuse to admit true premises
because of a foreseen conclusion. There are two
ways of defeating it, incorporated in the next
two sections.

4

❧❧❧

Conceal your game

If you want to draw a conclusion, you must not let it be foreseen, but you must get the premises admitted one by one, unobserved, mingling them here and there in your talk: otherwise, your opponent will attempt all sorts of chicanery. Or, if it is doubtful whether your opponent will admit them, you must advance the premises of these premises; that is to say, you must get the premises of several of them admitted in no definite order. In this way you conceal your strategy until you have obtained all the admissions that are necessary, and so reach your goal by making a circuit. It is a trick which needs no illustration.

5

⚜

False premises

To prove the truth of a proposition, you may also employ previous propositions that are not true, should your opponent refuse to admit the true ones (either because he fails to perceive their truth, or because he sees that the thesis immediately follows from them).

In that case the plan is to take propositions which are false in themselves but true for your opponent, and argue from the way in which he thinks. A true conclusion may follow from false premises, but not vice versa.

In the same fashion your opponent's false propositions may be refuted by other false propositions, which he, however, takes to be true. For it is with him that you have to do, and you must use the thoughts that he uses.

For instance, if he is a member of some sect to which you do not belong, you may employ the declared opinions of this sect against him, as principles.

6

❦

Postulate what has
to be proven

Another plan is to beg the question in disguise by postulating what has to be proven, either

(1) under another name; for instance, 'good repute' instead of 'honour'; 'virtue' instead of 'virginity', etc.; or by using such convertible terms as 'red-blooded animals' and 'vertebrates';
   or
(2) by making a general assumption covering the point in dispute: for instance, maintaining the uncertainty of medicine by postulating the uncertainty of all human

knowledge.

(3) If, vice versa, two things follow one from the other, and one is to be proved, you may postulate the other.

(4) If a general rule is to be proved, you may get your opponent to admit everyone of the particulars. (This is the reverse of the second.)

7

&ᴥ&

Yield admissions
through questions

Should the debate be conducted on somewhat
strict and formal lines, and there be a desire to
arrive at a very clear understanding, he who
states the proposition and wants to prove it
may proceed against his opponent by question, in order to show the truth of the statement from his opponent's admissions. (This
Socratic method was especially in use among
the ancients; and this and some of the tricks
following later on are akin to it.)

The plan is to ask your opponent a great
many wide-reaching questions at once, so as
to hide what you want to get admitted, and,
on the other hand, quickly propound the

argument resulting from his admissions. Those who are slow of understanding cannot follow accurately, and do not notice any mistakes or gaps there may be in the demonstration.

8

⁂

Make your opponent angry

For when he is angry he is incapable of judg-
ing aright and perceiving where his advantage
lies. You can make him angry by doing him
repeated injustice, or practising some kind of
chicanery, and being generally insolent.

9

꘠꘡꘢

Question in detouring order

Or you may put questions in an order different from that which the conclusion to be
drawn from them requires, and transpose
them, so as not to let him know at what you
are aiming. He can then take no precautions.

You may also use his answers for different
or even opposite conclusions according to
their character. This is akin to the trick of
masking your procedure.

[Cfr strategy 4]

10

&❦&

Take advantage of
the no-sayer

If you observe that your opponent returns a
negative answer on purpose to the questions
which, for the sake of your proposition, you
want him to answer in the affirmative, you
must ask the converse of the proposition, as
though it were that which you were anxious
to see affirmed. Or, at any rate, you may give
him his choice of both, so that he may not
perceive which of them you are asking him to
affirm.

11

֎

Generalise admissions of
specific cases

If you make an induction, and your opponent grants you the particular cases by which
it is to be supported, you must refrain from
asking him if he also admits the general truth
which issues from the particulars, but intro-
duce it afterwards as a settled and admitted
fact. In the meanwhile, he will himself come
to believe that he has admitted it, and the
same impression will be received by the audience. They will remember the many questions as to the particulars, and suppose that
they must, of course, have attained their end.

12

❧❧

Choose metaphors favourable to your proposition

If the conversation turns upon some general idea that has no particular name but requires some figurative or metaphorical designation, you must begin by choosing a metaphor that is favourable to your proposition.

For instance, the names used to denote the two political parties in Spain, *serviles* and *liberales*, are obviously chosen by the latter. The name *protestants* is chosen by themselves, and also the name *evangelicals*; but the catholics call them *heretics*. Similarly, in regard to the names of things which need a more exact and definite meaning. For example, if your opponent proposes an *alteration*, you can call it an *innovation,* as this is an invidious word. If you yourself make the proposal, it will be the converse. In the first case, you can call the principle 'the existing order', in the second, 'antiquated prejudice'. What an impartial man with no further purpose to serve would call 'public worship' or a 'system of religion', is described by an adherent as 'piety', 'godliness'; and by an opponent as 'bigotry', 'superstition'.

This is, at bottom, a subtle way of begging the question. What is sought to be proved is, first of all, inserted in the definition, whence it is then taken by mere analysis. What one man calls 'placing in safe custody', another calls 'throwing into prison'. A speaker often betrays his purpose beforehand by the names which he gives to things. One may talk of 'the clergy'; another, of 'the priests'.

Of all the tricks of controversy, this is the most frequent, and it is used instinctively. You hear of 'religious zeal', or 'fanaticism', a '*faux pas*', a 'piece of gallantry', or 'adultery'; an 'equivocal', or a 'bawdy' story; 'embarrassment', or 'bankruptcy'; 'through influence and connection', or by 'bribery and

Choose metaphors favourable to your proposition
nepotism'; 'sincere gratitude', or 'good pay'.

13

❧

Agree to reject the counter-argument

To make your opponent accept a proposition, you must give him the counter-proposition as well, leaving him his choice of the two. And you must render the contrast as glaring as you can, so that to avoid being paradoxical he will accept the proposition, which is thus made to look quite probable.

For instance, if you want to make him admit that a boy must do everything that his father tells him to do, ask him 'whether in all things we must obey or disobey our parents'. Or, if a thing is said to occur 'often', ask whether by 'often' you are to understand few or many cases; and he will say 'many'. It is as though you were to put grey next black, and call it white; or next white, and call it black.

14

ঌdownৎ

Claim victory despite defeat

This, which is an impudent trick, is played as follows. When your opponent has answered several of your questions without the answers turning out favourable to the conclusion at which you are aiming, advance the desired conclusion—although it does not in the least follow—as though it had been proved, and proclaim it in a tone of triumph.

If your opponent is shy or stupid, and you yourself possess a great deal of impudence and a good voice, the trick may easily succeed.

15

꩜

Use seemingly absurd propositions

If you have advanced a paradoxical proposition and find a difficulty in proving it, you may submit for your opponent's acceptance or rejection some true proposition—the truth of which, however, is not quite palpable—as though you wished to draw your proof from it. Should he reject it because he suspects a trick, you can obtain your triumph by showing how absurd he is; should he accept it, you have got reason on your side for the moment, and must now look about you.

Or else you can employ the previous trick as well, and maintain that your paradox is proved by the proposition which he has accepted. For this an extreme degree of impudence is required; but experience shows cases of it, and there are people who practise it by instinct.

16

꙰

Use your opponent's views

When your opponent advances a proposition, you must try to see whether it is not in some way—or only appears to be, if needs be—inconsistent with some other proposition which he has made or admitted, or with the principles of a school or sect which he has commended and approved, or with the actions of those who support the sect, or else of those who give it only an apparent and spurious support; or with his own actions or want of action.

For example, should he defend suicide, you may at once exclaim, 'Why don't you hang yourself?' Should he maintain that

Berlin is an unpleasant place to live in, you may say, 'Why don't you leave by the first train?' Such claptrap is always possible.

❋ ❋ ❋

The truth from which I draw my proof may be either:

(1) of an objective and universally valid character; in that case my proof is veracious. It is such proof alone that has any genuine validity.
Or
(2) it may be valid only for the person to whom I wish to prove my proposition, and with whom I am disputing. He has, that is to say, either taken up some position once for all as a prejudice, or hastily admitted it in the course of the dispute; and on this I ground my proof. In that case, it is a proof valid only for this particular man. I compel my opponent to grant my proposition, but I fail to establish it as a truth of universal validity. For example, if my opponent is a devotee of Kant's, and

I ground my proof on some utterance of that philosopher, it is a proof which in itself only applies to my opponent. If he is a Mohammedan, I may prove my point by reference to a passage in the Koran, and that is sufficient for him only.

17

❧

Defence through subtle distinction

If your opponent corners you with a counter-proof, you will often be able to save yourself by advancing some subtle distinction—which had not previously occurred to you—if the matter has a double application, or can be taken in any ambiguous sense.

18

❧❧

Interrupt, break-up, divert the debate

If you observe that your opponent has taken up a line of argument which will end in your defeat, you must not allow him to carry it to its conclusion, but interrupt the course of the dispute in time, or break it off altogether, or lead him away from the subject, and bring him to others. In short, you must effect a change of debate.

[Cfr strategy 29]

19

☙❧

Generalise the matter, then argue against it

Should your opponent expressly challenge you to produce any objection to some particular point in his argument and you have nothing much to say, you must try to give the matter a general turn, and then talk against that. If you are called upon to say why a particular physical hypothesis cannot be accepted, you may speak of the fallibility of human knowledge, and give various illustrations of it.

[*Cfr strategy 6*]

20

❧

Draw conclusions yourself

When you have elicited all your premises, and your opponent has admitted them, you must refrain from asking him for the conclusion, but draw it at once for yourself. In fact, even though one or other of the premises should be lacking, you may take it as though it too had been admitted, and draw the conclusion.

21

❧❧

Counter with an argument as bad as his

When your opponent uses a merely superficial argument and you see through it, you can, it is true, refute it by setting forth its captious character. But it is better to meet him with a counter-argument which is just as superficial, and so dispose of him. For it is with victory that you are concerned, and not with truth. If, for example, he adopts an argument that only applies to you, it is sufficient to take the force out of it by a counter-argument that applies only to him. In general, it is shorter to take this course if it is open to you.

22

❧❧❧

Beg the question

If your opponent requires you to admit something from which the point in dispute will immediately follow, you must refuse to do so, declaring that he is begging the question.

For he and the audience will regard a proposition which is near akin to the point in dispute as identical with it, and in this way you deprive him of his best argument.

23

❧❦

Make him exaggerate

Contradiction and contention irritate a man into exaggerating his statement. By contradicting your opponent you may drive him into extending beyond its proper limits a statement which, at all events within those limits and in itself, is true; and when you refute this exaggerated form of it, you look as though you had also refuted his original statement. Contrarily, you must take care not to allow yourself to be misled by contradiction into exaggerating or extending a statement of your own. It will often happen that your opponent will himself directly try to extend your statement further than you meant it;

here you must at once stop him, and bring
him back to the limits which you set up:
'that's what I said, and no more'.

24

☙❧

State a false syllogism

Your opponent puts forward a proposition, and by false inference and distortion of his ideas you force from it other propositions which it does not contain and he does not in the least mean; better yet, which are absurd or dangerous. It then looks as if his proposition gave rise to others which are inconsistent either with themselves or with some acknowledged truth, and so it appears to be in directly refuted.

25

❧❦

Find the instance to
the contrary

This is a case of the diversion by means of an *instance to the contrary*. With induction a great number of particular instances are required in order to establish it as a universal proposition; but with the diversion a single instance, to which the proposition does not apply, is all that is necessary to overthrow it.

This is a controversial method known as the *instance*. For example, 'all ruminants are horned' is a proposition which may be upset by the single instance of the camel.

The instance is a case in which a universal truth is sought to be applied, and something is inserted in the fundamental definition of it by which it is upset.

But there is room for mistake; and when this trick is employed by your opponent, you must observe:

(1) whether the example which he gives is really true; there are problems of which the only true solution is that the case in point is not true—for example, many miracles, ghost stories, and so on: and

(2) whether it really comes under the conception of the truth thus stated: for it may only appear to do so, and the matter is one to be settled by precise distinctions; and

(3) whether it is really inconsistent with this conception; for this again may be only an apparent inconsistency.

26

Turn the tables

A brilliant move is turning of the tables, by which your opponent's argument is turned against himself. He declares, for instance, 'So-and so is a child, you must make allowance for him'. You retort, 'Just because he is a child, I must correct him; otherwise he will persist in his bad habits'.

27

࿊࿊

Anger indicates a weak point

Should your opponent surprise you by becoming particularly angry at an argument, you must urge it with all the more zeal; not only because it is a good thing to make him angry, but because it may be presumed that you have here put your finger on the weak side of his case, and that just here he is more open to attack than even for the moment you perceive.

28

❧

Persuade the audience,
not the opponent

This is chiefly practicable in a dispute between scholars in the presence of the unlearned. If you have no refutation *whatsoever*, you can make one *aimed at the audience*; that is to say, you can start some invalid objection, which only an expert sees to be invalid. Though your opponent is an expert, those who form your audience are not, and accordingly, in their eyes, he is defeated, particularly if the objection which you make places him in any ridiculous light.

People are ready to laugh, and you have the laughers on your side. To show that your objection is an idle one, would require a long explanation on the part of your opponent, and a reference to the principles of the branch of knowledge in question, or to the elements of the matter which you are discussing; and people are not disposed to listen to it.

For example, your opponent states that in the original formation of a mountain-range the granite and other elements in its composition were, by reason of their high temperature, in a fluid or molten state; that the temperature must have amounted to some 480 degrees Fahrenheit; and that when the mass took shape it was covered by the sea. You reply that at that temperature—indeed, long before it had been reached, namely, at 212 degrees Fahrenheit—the sea would have been boiled away, and spread through the air in the form of steam. At this the audience laughs. To refute the objection, your opponent would have to show that the boiling-point depends not only on the degree of warmth, but also on the atmospheric pressure; and that as soon as about half the sea-water had gone off in the shape of steam, this pressure would be so greatly increased that the rest of it would fail to boil even at a temperature of 480 degrees. He is debarred from giving this explanation, as it would require a treatise to demonstrate the matter to those who had no acquaintance with physics.

29

⊱∽⊰

Diversion

If you find that you are being worsted, you can make a *diversion*—that is, you can suddenly begin to talk of something else, as though it had a bearing on the matter in dispute, and afforded an argument against your opponent. This may be done without presumption if the diversion has, in fact, some general bearing on the matter; but it is a piece of impudence if it has nothing to do with the case, and is only brought in by way of attacking your opponent.

For example, I praise the system prevailing in China, where there is no such thing as hereditary nobility, and offices are bestowed only on those who succeed in competitive examinations. My opponent argues that learning, as little as the privilege of birth (of which he has a high opinion), fits a man for office. We debated the issue, and he got the worst of it. Then he made a diversion, and declared that in China all ranks were punished with the bastinado*, which he connected with the immoderate indulgence in tea, and proceeded to make both of them a subject of reproach to the Chinese.

To follow him into all this would have been to allow oneself to be drawn into a surrender of the victory which had already been won.

The diversion is mere impudence if it completely abandons the point in dispute, and raises, for instance, some such objection as 'Yes, and you also said just now', and so on. For then the argument becomes to some extent personal; of the kind which will be treated of in the last section.

How very innate this trick is, may be seen in every quarrel between common people. If one of the parties makes some personal reproach against the other, the latter, instead of answering it by refuting it, allows it to stand—as it were, admits it; and replies by reproaching his antagonist on some other ground. This is the strategy that Scipio pursued when he attacked the Carthaginians, not in Italy, but in Africa.

In war, diversions of this kind may be profitable; but in a quarrel they are poor expedients, because the attacks remain standing, and those who look on hear the worst that can be said of both parties. It is a trick that should be used only *faute de mieux*.

[*Cfr strategy 18*]

* Cudgel.

30

❧

Appeal to authority rather than reason

It consists of making an appeal to authority rather than reason, using such an authority as may suit the degree of knowledge possessed by your opponent.

Every man prefers belief to the exercise of judgement, says Seneca. It is therefore an easy matter if you have an authority on your side which your opponent respects. The more limited his capacity and knowledge, the greater is the number of the authorities who weigh with him. But if his capacity and knowledge are of a high order, there are very few; indeed, hardly any at all. He may, perhaps, admit the authority of professional men

the elect who say with Plato *tois pollois polla dokei*; which means that the public has a good many bees in its bonnet, and that it would be a tall order to get at them.

To speak seriously, the universality of an opinion is no proof. In fact, it is not even a probability that the opinion is right.

Those who maintain that it is so must assume:

(1) that length of time deprives a universal opinion of its demonstrative force, as otherwise all the old errors which were once universally held to be true would have to be recalled; for instance, the Ptolemaic system would have to be restored, or Catholicism re-established in all Protestant countries.

They must assume:

(2) that distance of space has the same effect; otherwise the respective universality of opinion among the adherents of Buddhism, Christianity, and Islam will put them in a difficulty.

When we come to look into the matter,

so-called universal opinion is the opinion of two or three persons. We should be persuaded of this if we could see the way in which it really arises.

We should find that it is two or three persons who, in the first instance, accepted it, or advanced and maintained it; and of whom people were so good as to believe that they had thoroughly tested it. Then a few other persons, persuaded beforehand that the first were men of the requisite capacity, also accepted the opinion. These, again, were trusted by many others, whose laziness prompted them to think that it was better to believe at once than to go through the troublesome task of testing the matter for themselves. Thus the number of these lazy and credulous adherents grew from day to day. For the opinion had no sooner obtained a fair measure of support than its further supporters attributed this to the fact that the opinion could only have obtained it by the cogency of its arguments. The remainder were then compelled to grant what was universally granted, so as not to pass for unruly persons who resisted opinions which everyone accepted, or pert fellows who thought themselves cleverer than any one else.

When opinion reaches this stage, adhesion becomes a duty. Henceforward the few who are capable of forming a judgement hold their peace. Those who venture to speak are entirely incapable of forming any opinions or any judgement of their own, being merely the echo of others' opinions. Nevertheless, they defend them with all the greater zeal and intolerance. For what they hate in people who think differently is not so much the different opinions which they have as the presumption of wanting to form their own judgement. In short, there are very few who can think, but every man wants to have an opinion; and what remains but to take it ready-made from others, instead of forming opinions for himself?

Since this is what happens, where is the value of the opinion even of a hundred millions?

It is no more established than an historical fact reported by a hundred chroniclers who can be proved to have plagiarised it from one another; the opinion in the end being traceable to a single individual.* It is all what I say, what you say, and, finally, what he says; and the whole of it is nothing but a series of assertions:

Dico ego, tu dicis, sed denique dixit et ille;
Dictaque post toties, nil nisi dicta vides.

Nevertheless, in a dispute with ordinary people, we may employ universal opinion as an authority. For it will generally be found that when two of them are fighting, that is the weapon which both of them choose as a means of attack. If a man of the better sort has to deal with them, it is most advisable for him to condescend to the use of this weapon too, and to select such authorities as will make an impression on his opponent's weak side. For, *by definition*, ordinary man is as insensible to all rational argument as a horny-hided Siegfried, dipped in the flood of incapacity, and unable to think or judge.

Before a court of law the dispute is one between authorities alone—such authoritative statements, I mean, as are laid down by legal experts. The exercise of judgement consists in discovering what law or authority applies to the case in question. There is, however, plenty of room for dialectic. Should the case in question and the law not really fit each other, they can, if necessary, be twisted until they appear to do so, or vice versa.

* See Bayle's *Pensées sur les Comètes*, i., p. 10.

31

※

This is beyond me

If you know that you have no reply to the arguments which your opponent advances, you may, by a fine stroke of irony, declare yourself to be an incompetent judge: 'What you now say passes my poor powers of comprehension. It may be all very true, but I can't understand it, and I refrain from any expression of opinion on it.'

In this way you insinuate to the bystanders, with whom you are in good repute, that what your opponent says is nonsense. Thus, when Kant's *Kritik* appeared—or, rather, when it began to make a noise in the world—many professors of the old eclec-

tic school declared that they failed to understand it, in the belief that their failure settled
the business. But when the adherents of the
new school proved to them that they were
quite right, and had really failed to understand it, they were in a very bad temper.

This is a trick which may be used only
when you are quite sure that the audience
thinks much better of you than of your opponent. A professor, for instance, may try it on
a student.

Strictly speaking, it is a case of the preced-
ing trick: it is a particularly malicious assertion of one's own authority, instead of giving
reasons.

The counter-trick is to say: 'I beg your par-
don; but, with your penetrating intellect, it
must be very easy for you to understand anything; and it can only be my poor statement
of the matter that is at fault'; and then go on
to rub it into him until he understands it, and
sees for himself that it was really his own
fault alone.

In this way you parry his attack. With the
greatest politeness he wanted to insinuate that
you were talking nonsense. And you, with

This is beyond me

equal courtesy, prove to him that he is a fool.

32

❧

Put his thesis into some odious category

If you are confronted with an assertion, there is a short way of getting rid of it, or, at any rate, of throwing suspicion on it, by putting it into some odious category; even though the connection is only apparent, or else of a loose character.

You can say, for instance, 'That is Manichaeism' or 'It is Arianism', or 'Pelagianism', or 'Idealism', or 'Spinozism', or 'Pantheism', or 'Brownianism', or 'Naturalism', or 'Atheism', or 'Rationalism', 'Spiritualism', 'Mysticism', and so on.

In making an objection of this kind, you take it for granted:

(1) that the assertion in question is identical with, or is at least contained in, the category cited—that is to say, you cry out, 'Oh, I have heard that before';
and

(2) that the system referred to has been entirely refuted, and does not contain a word of truth.

33

❧

It applies in theory,
but not in practice

'That's all very well in theory, but it won't
do in practice.' In this sophism you admit the
premises but deny the conclusion, in contradiction with a well-known rule of logic. The
assertion is based upon an impossibility: what
is right in theory must work in practice; and
if it does not, there is a mistake in the theory;
something has been overlooked and not
allowed for; and, consequently, what is
wrong in practice is wrong in theory too.

34

❧☙

Don't let him off the hook

When you state a question or an argument,
and your opponent gives you no direct
answer or reply, but evades it by a counter-
question or an indirect answer (or some assertion which has no bearing on the matter, and,
generally, tries to turn the subject), it is a sure
sign that you have touched a weak spot,
sometimes without knowing it. You have, as
it were, reduced him to silence. You must,
therefore, urge the point all the more, and
not let your opponent evade it, even when
you do not know where the weakness which
you have hit upon really lies.

35

❦

Will is more effective
than insight

There is another trick which, as soon as it is practicable, makes all others unnecessary. Instead of working on your opponent's intellect by argument, work on his will by motive. He, and also the audience if they have similar interests, will at once be won over to your opinion—even though you got it out of a lunatic asylum. As a general rule, half an ounce of will is more effective than a hundred-weight of insight and intelligence.

This, it is true, can be done only under particuliar circumstances. If you succeed in making your opponent feel that his opinion—should it prove true—will be distinctly prejudicial to his interest, he will let it drop like a hot potato, and feel that it was very imprudent to take it up.

A clergyman, for instance, is defending some philosophical dogma; you make him realise the fact that it is in immediate contradiction with one of the fundamental doctrines of his Church, and he abandons it.

A landed proprietor maintains that the use of machinery in agricultural operations, as practised in England, is an excellent institution, since an engine does the work of many men. You give him to understand that it will not be very long before carriages are also worked by steam, and that the value of his large stud will be greatly depreciated. You will see what he will then say.

In such cases every man feels how thoughtless it is to sanction a law unjust to himself! Nor is it any different if the bystanders, but not your opponent, belong to the same sect, guild, industry, club, etc., as yourself.

Let his thesis be never so true. As soon as you hint that it is prejudicial to the common interests of the said society, all the bystanders will find that your opponent's arguments, however excellent they be, are weak and contemptible; and that yours, on the other hand, though they were random conjecture, are correct and to the point; you will have a chorus of loud approval on your side.

Your opponent will be driven out of the field with ignominy. In fact, the bystanders will believe, as a rule, that they have agreed with you out of pure conviction. For what is not to our interest mostly seems absurd to us; our intellect being no *siccum lumen*. This trick might be called 'taking the tree by its root'.

36

❧

The Vicar of Wakefield

You may also puzzle and bewilder your opponent by mere bombast; and the trick is possible, because man generally supposes that there must be some meaning in words:

*Gewöhnlich glaubt der Mensch, wenn er
nur Worte hort,
Es musse sich dabei doch auch was
denken lassen.**

If he is secretly conscious of his own weakness—and accustomed to hear much that he does not understand, and to make as though he did—you can easily impose upon him by some serious fooling that sounds very deep or learned, and deprives him of hearing, sight, and thought; and by giving out that it is the most indisputable proof of what you assert. It is a well-known fact that in recent times some philosophers have practised this trick on the whole of the public with the most brilliant success.

But since present examples are odious, we may refer to *The Vicar of Wakefield* for an old one.

* When man hears a few spoken words, he assumes they must be meaningful.

37

꧁꧂

A faulty proof refutes
his whole position

Should your opponent be in the right, but, luckily for your contention, choose a faulty proof, you can easily manage to refute it, and then claim that you have thus refuted his whole position. This is a trick which ought to be one of the first. It is, at bottom, an expedient by which an argument against the opponent himself is put forward as an argument that applies in general against his proposition.

If no accurate proof occurs to him or to the bystanders, you will have won the day.

For example, if a man advances the ontological argument by way of proving God's existence, you can get the best of him, for the ontological argument may easily be refuted. This is the way in which bad advocates lose a good case, by trying to justify it by an authority which does not fit it, when no fitting one occurs to them.

38

☙❧

The ultimate strategy

A last trick is to become personal, insulting, rude, as soon as you perceive that your opponent has the upper hand, and that you are going to come off worst.

It consists in passing from the subject of dispute, as from a lost game, to the disputant himself, and in some way attacking his person.

It may be called the *argumentum ad personam*—to distinguish it from other arguments which pass from the objective discussion of the subject, pure and simple, to statements or admissions which your opponent has made in regard to it.

But in becoming personal you leave the subject altogether, and turn your attack to his person (*ad personam*), by remarks of an offensive and spiteful character. It is an appeal from the virtues of the intellect to the virtues of the body, or to mere animalism.

This is a very popular trick, because everyone is able to carry it into effect; and so it is of frequent application.

Now the question is, what counter-trick is available to the other party? For if he has recourse to the same rule, there will be blows, or a duel, or an action for slander.

It would be a great mistake to suppose that it is sufficient not to become personal yourself. By showing a man quite quietly that he is wrong, and that what he says and thinks is incorrect—a process which occurs in every dialectical victory—you embitter him more than if you use some rude or insulting expression.

Why is this?

Because, as Hobbes observes, all mental pleasure consists in being able to compare oneself with others to one's own advantage. Nothing is of greater moment to a man than the gratification of his vanity, and no wound is more painful than that which is inflicted on it.

Hence such phrases as 'Death before dishonour', and so on. The gratification of vanity arises mainly by comparison of oneself with others, in every respect, but chiefly in respect of one's intellectual powers; and so the most effective and the strongest gratification of it is to be found in controversy. Hence the embitterment of defeat, apart from any question of injustice; and hence recourse to that last weapon, that last trick, which you cannot evade by mere politeness.

A cool demeanour may, however, help you here. As soon as your opponent becomes personal, you quietly reply, 'That has no bearing on the point in dispute', and immediately bring the conversation back to it, and continue to show him that he is wrong, without taking any notice of his insults. Say, as Themistocles said to Eurybiades, 'Strike, but hear me.'

But such demeanour is not given to everyone.

❋ ❋ ❋

As a sharpening of wits, controversy is often, indeed, of mutual advantage, in order to correct one's thoughts and awaken new views.

But in learning and in mental power both disputants must be tolerably equal. If one of them lacks learning, he will fail to understand the other, as he is not on the same level with his antagonist. If he lacks mental power, he will be embittered, and led into dishonest tricks, and end by being rude.

The only safe rule, therefore, is not to dispute with the first person you meet, but only with those of your acquaintance of whom you know that they possess sufficient intelligence and self-respect not to advance absurdities; to appeal to reason and not to authority, and to listen to reason and yield to it; and, finally, to cherish truth, to be willing to accept reason even from an opponent, and to be just enough to bear being proved to be in the wrong, should truth lie with him.

From this it follows that scarcely one man in a hundred is worth your disputing with him.

You may let the remainder say what they please, for everyone is at liberty to be a fool. Remember what Voltaire says: La paix vaut encore mieux que la verité. *Remember also an Arab proverb which tells us that on the tree of silence there hangs its fruit, which is peace.*

I
Appendix

The ancients used logic and dialectic as synonymous terms, although *logizesthai*, 'to think over, to consider, to calculate', and *dialegesthai*, 'to converse', are two very different things.

The name dialectic was, as we are informed by Diogenes Laertius, first used by Plato; and in the *Phaedrus, Sophist, Republic*, bk. vii., and elsewhere, we find that by dialectic he means the regular employment of the reason, and skill in the practice of it. Aristotle also uses the word in this sense; but, according to Laurentius Valla, he was the first to use logic too in a similar way. Dialectic, therefore, seems to be an older word than logic. Cicero and Quintilian use the words in the same general way.

This use of the words as synonymous terms lasted through the Middle Ages into modern times; in fact, until the present day. But more recently, and in particular by Kant, dialectic has often been employed in a bad sense, as meaning 'the art of sophistical controversy'; and hence logic has been preferred, as of the two the more innocent designation. Nevertheless, both originally meant the same thing; and in the last few years they have again been recognised as synonymous.

II
Appendix

It is a pity that the words have thus been used from of old, and that I am not quite at liberty to distinguish their meanings. Otherwise, I should have preferred to define *logic* (from *logos*, 'word' and 'reason', which are inseparable) as 'the science of the laws of thought, that is, of the method of reason'; and *dialectic* (from *dialegesthai*, 'to converse'—and every conversation communicates either facts or opinions, that is to say, it is historical or deliberative) as 'the art of disputation', in the modern sense of the word. It is clear, then, that logic deals with a subject of a purely *a priori* character, separable in definition from experience, namely, the laws of thought, the process of reason or the *logos*; the laws, that is, which reason follows when it is left to itself and not hindered, as in the case of solitary thought on the part of a rational being who is in no way misled. dialectic, on the other hand, would treat of the intercourse between two rational beings who, because they are rational, ought to think in common, but who, as soon as they cease to agree like two clocks keeping exactly the same time, create a disputation, or intellectual contest. Regarded as purely rational beings, the individuals would, I say, necessarily be in agreement, and their variation springs from the difference essential to individuality; in other words, it is drawn from experience.

Logic, therefore, as the science of thought, or the science of the process of pure reason, should be capable of being constructed *a priori*. dialectic, for the most part, can be constructed only *a posteriori*; that is to say, we may learn its rules by an experiential knowledge of the disturbance which pure thought suffers through the difference of individuality manifested in the intercourse between two rational beings, and also by acquaintance with the means which disputants adopt in order to make good against one another their own individual thought, and to show that it is pure and objective. For human nature is such that if A and B are engaged in thinking in common, and are communicating their opinions to one another on any subject, so long as it is not a mere fact of history, and A perceives that B's thoughts on one end the same subject are not the same as his own, he does not begin by revising his own process of thinking, so as to discover any mistake which he may have made, but he assumes that the mistake has occurred in B's. In other words, man is naturally obstinate; and this quality in him is attended with certain results, treated of in the branch of knowledge which I should like to call dialectic, but which, in order to avoid misunderstanding, I shall call controversial or eristical dialectic. Accordingly, it is the branch of knowledge which treats of the obstinacy natural to man.

III
Appendix

First of all, we must consider the essential nature of every dispute. What is it that really takes place.

Our opponent has stated a thesis (or we ourselves). There are two modes of refuting it, and two courses that we may pursue.

I.

The modes are (1) We may show either that the proposition is not in accordance with the objective truth (*ad rem*); (2) or that it is inconsistent with other statements or admissions of our opponent, *i.e.*, with truth as it appears to him (*ad hominem*).

The latter mode makes no difference whatever to the objective truth of the matter.

II.

The two courses that we may pursue are (1) the direct, and (2) the indirect refutation. The direct course attacks the reason for the thesis; the indirect, its results. The direct refutation shows that the thesis is not true; the indirect, that it cannot be true.

The direct course is a two-fold procedure. Either we may show that the reasons for the statement are false or we may admit the premises, but show that the statement does not follow from them; that is, we attack the conclusion.

The direct refutation makes use either of *diversion*, or of *instance*.

(a) *The diversion*. We accept our opponent's proposition as true, and then show what follows from it when we bring it into connection with some other proposition acknowledged to be true. We use the two as the premises of a conclusion which is manifestly false,* or other statements of our opponent himself.

(b) *The instance, or the example to the contrary.*
This consists in refuting the general proposition by reference to cases which are
included in it, but to which it does not
apply.

Such is the framework or skeleton of all
forms of disputation; for to this every kind of
controversy may be ultimately reduced.
The whole of a controversy may, however, actually proceed in the manner described,
or only appear to do so; and it may be supported by genuine or spurious arguments. It
is just because it is not easy to make out the
truth in regard to this matter, that debates are
so long and so obstinate.

Nor can we, in ordering the argument,
separate actual from apparent truth. Even the
disputants are not certain about it beforehand. Therefore I shall describe the various
tricks without regard to questions of objective truth or falsity; for that is a matter on
which we have no assurance, and which cannot be determined previously.

Schopenhauer's Pessimism

A.C. Grayling

The pessimistic cast of Schopenhauer's attitude to human nature is an instance of the general pessimism of his philosophy. Starting from Kant's distinction between phenomenal and noumenal reality (the former being reality as it is experienced by us, the latter being reality as it is in itself), he argued that Kant was wrong to say the latter is completely inaccessible, for we encounter it in the form of our will—our volition—which is the in-itself of our own phenomenal being. And by extension from this, he said, we can recognise that will is the inner essence of all reality.

Because will is a non-rational, striving

force which operates blindly, without aim or purpose, it follows that Hegel's assertion that the 'real is the rational' is false. It also follows that enslavement to the will's blind strivings is, as recognised and made central in the ethics of the Upanishads and Buddhist texts which so influenced Schopenhauer, the reason why life fundamentally consists in suffering. This, Schopenhauer thought, is the great truth of things. Liberation from this suffering can be achieved only by the will 'turning and denying itself', that is, by achieving a cessation of desire and attachment to phenomenal things.

It is a corollary of this view that Schopenhauer's idea of human nature is a negative one. He vigorously contested the idea that ethics should be based on the idea of human dignity as what commands respectful and considerate treatment between people; per contra, any human being is such that 'the wickedness of his will, the limitation of his intellect and the perversity of his notions should make us despise him.' The basis of our ethical attitude should instead be, Schopenhauer says, our perception only of another's 'sufferings, his need, anxiety and pain. We shall then always feel in sympathy with him, akin to him, and instead of hatred or contempt, we will feel compassion.' Nevertheless, the endemic wickedness and perversity of human nature, an artefact of the blind will that forces everything from within, among other things is what makes people seek victory in argument rather than truth; therefore, Schopenhauer says, be equipped to do likewise, and to win.

Translator's Note

The volume now before the reader is a tardy addition to a series in which I have endeavoured to present Schopenhauer's minor writings in an adequate form.

Its contents are drawn entirely from his posthumous papers. A selection of them was given to the world some three of four years after his death by his friend and literary executor, Julius Frauenstaedt, who for this and other offices of piety, has received less recognition than he deserves. The papers then published have recently been issued afresh, with considerable additions and corrections, by Dr Eduard Grisebach, who is also entitled to gratitude for the care with which he has followed the text of the manuscripts, now in the Royal Library at Berlin, and for having drawn attention—although in terms that are unnecessarily severe—to a number of faults and failings on the part of the previous editor.

The fact that all Schopenhauer's works, together with a volume of his correspondence, may now be obtained in a certain cheap collection of the best national and foreign literature displayed in almost every bookshop in Germany, is sufficient evidence that in his own country the writer's popularity is still very great; nor does the demand for translations indicate that his fame has at all diminished abroad. The favour with which the new edition of his posthumous papers has been received induces me, therefore, to resume a task which I thought, five years ago, that I had finally completed; and it is my intention to bring out one more volume, selected partly from these papers and partly from his *Parerga*.

A small part of the essay on *The Art of Controversy* was published in Schopenhauer's lifetime, in the chapter of the *Parerga* headed

Zur Logik und Dialektik. The intelligent reader will discover that a good deal of its contents is of an ironical character. As regards the last three essays I must observe that I have omitted such passages as appear to be no longer of any general interest or otherwise unsuitable. I must also confess to having taken one or two liberties with the titles, in order that they may the more effectively fulfil the purpose for which titles exist. In other respects I have adhered to the original with the kind of fidelity which aims at producing an impression as nearly as possible similar to that produced by the original.

T. Bailey Saunders

Publisher's Note

Apart from scholars, few readers will nowadays be familiar with the debate on sophistry that started in ancient Greece. Continued in the confinement of university studies to the present day, it still follows lines carved out at that time. Schopenhauer's novel contribution, however, contains much that will intrigue the modern reader, given the ever growing importance of public debating on TV and radio. Schopenhauer's posthumous work is known in German as *Die Kunst Recht zu Behalten*. In France it is appropriately translated as *L'Art d'avoir toujours raison*,* a convention adopted here. This edited version of the work excludes references in the original text and is based on the English translation by T. Bailey Saunders, last published by Macmillan in 1896 as *The Art of Controversy*. The unedited translation by Bailey Saunders is available from info@gibsonsquare.com. It varies on a number of points from the published German text, introducing several cuts. Interested readers with German may therefore also want to consult Schopenhauer's work in the original language.

* Recently by Mille et Une Nuits, 2000.